SPIRITUAL VALUE

Stephen Kaung

ISBN: 978-1-942521-43-3

Available from:

Christian Testimony Ministry
4424 Huguenot Road
Richmond, Virginia 23235

www.christiantestimonyministry.com

Printed in USA

CONTENTS

THE PRINCIPLE OF SPIRITUAL VALUE

Matthew 16:26—For what does a man profit, if he should gain the whole world and suffer the loss of his soul? or what shall a man give in exchange for his soul?

Shall we pray:

Dear heavenly Father, we do rejoice in Thy presence. We praise and thank Thee for Thy beloved Son, our Lord Jesus. We thank Thee for revealing Thy Son in us. Lord, our prayer before Thee this morning is that He may be magnified in us. We ask that Thou would open our eyes through Thy word that we may see what Thy beloved Son sees and we will be what Thy beloved Son wants us to be. We just commit this time into Your hands, trusting Thee for Thy speaking and for Thy working in us. And to Thee we give glory. In Thy precious name. Amen.

In the verse that we have just read, our Lord Jesus Himself tells us the importance of spiritual value. He said, "What does a man profit if he should gain the whole world and suffer the loss of his soul?" Our Lord put the whole world on one side, and that is probably more than anyone can imagine. How much is the whole world? The world that we know or we are seeking after, probably is a little bit of the world, but it is already the whole world to us. Yet, our Lord Jesus actually put the whole world on one side. Everything that the world is—whatever you can think of or even imagine that the world is—the Lord put on one side. Then, on the other side, He puts your soul, and He said, "What would it profit you if you gain the whole world and lose your soul?" In other words, in the eyes of our Lord a soul is of more value, is much more valuable than the whole world. Spiritual things are much more valuable than earthly things, but to our natural minds it is very difficult to accept this because we think the world is full of value and the soul has little value. Usually, we despise things that are spiritual. To us they are vague, abstract, but the world seems very real and very valuable to us. So our thinking, usually, is very different from the thinking of our Lord Jesus.

WHO DETERMINES VALUE?

We would like to consider together before the Lord: What is value? Where does value come from? Who decides what the value is? I personally believe that God determines value. God Himself is value and out of Him He created all things. Everything that He creates has a value because it manifests something of God. When we look at His created things, we can see His divinity and His power, and that expression of His divinity and His power is the value. He created man, and why is man more valuable than the whole world to Him? It is because He created man in His own image. In other words, because there is more of God in man when created than in the other things, therefore, man is more valuable than the world. In other words, we need to understand the very concept of value. Value is not something that we put on a thing. True value is set by God. God puts a value in a thing and that is its intrinsic value. Different things have different value, but there is no thing, nothing, that has no value of any kind because it comes out of God. It is very true that spiritual things

3

have more value than earthly things because God is Spirit. The closer it is to God, the more valuable that thing is; the more it manifests God, the more there is of true value.

I believe that in the beginning all things worked together for good. In other words, there was nothing, whether spiritual or physical, that was really working against each other. I believe in the beginning everything worked together for the glory of God, whether it was heavenly or whether it was earthly, whether it was spiritual or whether it was physical. They all worked together for the glory of God. That is what you see in the garden of Eden before sin entered into the world. God planted a beautiful garden, a garden of pleasure, and he put man in that garden. In that garden were all kinds of fruit trees that were good to look at and good to eat. God provided all these physical things for man to live by and to enjoy, and in the midst of the garden God put the tree of life. There is nothing better than the tree of life because the tree of life actually is a tree in which the life of God dwells, and if you eat the tree of life you receive the very divine life of God. What can be more excellent than that tree!

Also, by the side of it was the tree of the knowledge of good and evil. Now we often think that the tree of the knowledge of good and evil was a bad tree. Do you think God would put anything bad in the garden of Eden? As a matter of fact, the tree of the knowledge of good and evil is better than all the other trees except the tree of life because all the other trees are for physical needs. God created us with a body, so He provided us with the means of sustaining this physical body. He is love. The tree of the knowledge of good and evil actually is the food of the soul. The soul is more important than the body. We need knowledge—knowledge of good and evil which is rational, ethical knowledge. As a matter of fact, this kind of knowledge is the highest knowledge in the world. It is higher than scientific knowledge or speculative knowledge. It is moral knowledge. That is the highest kind of knowledge; it is the food for the soul. But of course the Lord said, "Of all of the trees in the garden you can freely eat, but of the tree of the knowledge of good and evil you should not eat, because on the day that you eat thereof you shall surely die" (see Genesis 2:17).

MAN'S CHOICE

I think the tree itself is not a bad tree but God put it there for two reasons. Number one: God put the tree of the knowledge of good and evil there in order that man may choose what they wanted to be, in order that man could decide for themselves what was more valuable. God set the value there but would man agree with God as to His value? God gave man a choice, an exercise of free will to show whether he wanted the best or whether he wanted the better; but the better becomes the enemy of the best. Without the life of God, knowledge will kill because you know what is right but you cannot do it; you know what is wrong but you do it. How much better it is if you do not have that kind of knowledge. I think the babies are more fortunate because when they are doing things, they do not have that knowledge of good and evil; they are not responsible. God does not hold them responsible; but with grown ups, it is different.

God holds us responsible, and in our experience we know that knowledge really kills. It condemns us. It brings us to death. Very true. Sometimes I wonder (of course, this is speculative) if Adam had eaten the tree of life first, would God continue to forbid him to eat the tree of the knowledge of good and evil? I do not know. But I will say that all things do work together for good, and in our own experience we find it out. Without the life of God this knowledge of good and evil is killing, but with the life of God this knowledge of good and evil will bring glory to God. So you see God put that tree in the garden to give man an opportunity to decide for himself what is most valuable to him—God or himself.

MAN IS OVER ALL BUT UNDER ONE

The second reason God gave such a commandment, such a prohibition, was to show man that even though he is over all things, he is under God. In that garden, they could eat of every tree with only one limitation. How wide that liberty was! But God put that limitation upon man to remind him he was under God. God gave man the dominion over the fowls of the air, the animals on the earth, the creeping things, and the fishes in the sea. Man is above all God's created things on earth but God wanted to remind man that even though he is above all, he is under One.

When you are above all, you tend to forget that you are below One. That is a great temptation, and probably that is the reason why Lucifer fell because in a sense he was created the most beautiful archangel—above all, but he forgot he was below One. Maybe, for that reason God used it to remind man: "Now remember this: you are below One. That is your place, and if you remain in your place, you will be above all, but if you do not remain in your place you will lose everything."

THE WRONG CHOICE

Before sin entered into this world, everything that God created had its invested value, and all worked together for the glory of God. Everything was in its proper place, its proper order, but unfortunately, our forefathers made the wrong choice. In other words, our forefathers Adam and Eve saw the two trees there but they chose their own lives instead of choosing God. Their own souls were more important, more valuable to them than having God to be their life. They wanted to develop their own soul life to make them feel great. They did not want to depend upon God but they would be as gods themselves. They were tempted by the enemy. They fell into his trap and in trying to gain their souls, they lost their souls.

Not only did Adam and Eve lose their souls, but they lost their world, too. Since then, the enemy took hold of the world, the created things that God had entrusted to man to have dominion over, to rule for God, to bring everything to the feet of God for His glory. Because man fell and surrendered himself to the enemy, Satan took the world from man, not by right but by a devious way, and he became the ruler of this world. He took God's created things, organized them together, made them a system, a cosmos over which he ruled, and he used the world, the things of this world that God had created, to oppose God. In other words, under his control, the world has a negative value instead of a positive value. The value has changed. There is nothing wrong with eating and drinking. We have to eat. We have to drink; that is legitimate. But the enemy has made eating and drinking the lust of the flesh, the lust of the eye, and the pride of life. The world is now against our spiritual life, instead of supporting our spiritual life. The nature has changed. The value has changed. It does not have a positive value anymore; its value is negative.

The same thing happened to our soul. Instead of using our soul to love God with all our soul, to will God's will, and to think of the things above, now this soul has fallen. We become self-centered, trying to enrich our soul-life by seeking the things of the world, but in doing that we not only will not have the world, we will even lose our soul-life. So you remember our Lord Jesus said to His disciples, "Verily, verily, I say unto you, if you lose your soul-life for My sake and the gospel's sake, you shall gain your soul-life, but if you should gain your soul-life you will lose it." Value has changed.

MAN'S SENSE OF TRUE VALUE WAS LOST

This whole concept of value is not what it ought to be. Our sense of value has lost its direction. We value the things that are hurtful to our spiritual life and we despise the things that are helpful to our spiritual life. Even though we may sometimes mentally agree with what is more valuable, yet for us to really value what should be valued, we cannot do it.

Also, because there is value, therefore there is a cost. Anything that has a value demands a price, a cost. So our Lord Jesus said, "What profit do you really get if you gain the whole world and lose your soul?" In other words, if you want the world, your soul will be the price for it. You do not gain the world freely. God gave the world to us for free, but the enemy will not give you the world for free. If you want to have the world, he says, "Give me your soul."

What profit is that? Even if you gain the whole world, how long will you have it? But your soul will continue. It is an exchange. In this world, today, you do not get anything for free. It

11

is an exchange. You exchange your soul for the world and the Lord says it is a loss, not a gain. That is the reason why our Lord Jesus came into this world.

OUR LORD JESUS SHOWED US REAL VALUE

So far as we human beings are concerned, we are fallen. Our sense of value is totally distorted, upside down. We value the things that we shouldn't and we despise the things that we should treasure. That is the way we were. It is not just a matter of a little knowledge, a little teaching; there must be a drastic change. That is the reason why our Lord Jesus came into this world. He came into this world to show us what real value is. His whole life is a demonstration of spiritual value. In His whole life He was not seeking for earthly gain. He had opportunities, even when He was in the wilderness being tempted by Satan. Satan showed Him the whole world, all the riches of the whole world, and Satan said, "Just bow to me and it is all Yours. Give me Your soul and all this will be Yours." Our forefather, Adam, fell; when he was tempted, he did it. Thank God for the second Man. He had the whole world given to Him and He said, "It is written, 'You shall worship the Lord your God and serve Him alone.'" In other words, He chose God, the supreme value of the universe. He rejected the world and saved His soul.

When our Lord Jesus was on earth, in the beginning people flocked to Him when He preached. They loved to hear Him. They said He spoke differently from the Pharisees and the scribes because He spoke with authority. He healed the sick. He was a friend of the sinners. In the beginning, they had the idea that He probably was the Messiah, especially when He used the five loaves and two fishes to feed five thousand. They said, "Well, He must be the Messiah," and they wanted to force Him to be King. Now you do not need to force anyone to be king. They will force their way through to be king. But you find they tried to force the Lord to be king, and the Lord sent them away. He even sent His disciples away because His disciples would have liked it very much if He would be king; and He went to the mountain to pray.

He was demonstrating to the world what true value is. God is THE value. Anything outside of God, no matter how good it may look, has no value; it is negative value. Only when things are in God is the value preserved. So you find that our Lord Jesus' whole principle of living was the Father's will. He would not lift His finger to do a thing for Himself. During the temptation He had fasted forty days and forty nights and He was hungry because He was human. The enemy said, "If you are the Son of God, turn the stone into bread. You can do it."

Of course He could. But then our Lord said, "It is written, 'Man shall not live by bread alone but by every word that proceeds from the mouth of God.'" He would rather be hungry than to do something against the will of God because He valued God's will more than His own life.

When the children of Israel saw that He was different, that He did not want to be king, that He had no ambition for this world and He was only trying to bring people to God for their spiritual good, they were tired of Him; they rejected Him. So our Lord retreated to the border of Caesarea-

Philippi, which is a Gentile city, and during His rejection, He asked His disciples: "Who do men say that I, the Son of man, am?" Of course, they gave Him all the good reports. Some said, "You are John the Baptist come to life." Now we know that Herod did have that thought. After he murdered John the Baptist, his conscience bothered him, and when he heard about Jesus, he said, "John the Baptist has come back to life." Some said, "You are Elias, that great prophet; You are Jeremiah"; because our Lord wept.

Isn't it strange that you cannot find a place in the Bible where the Lord laughed? But a number of times He wept, He groaned. Now that does not mean our Lord lived a very unhappy life because joy and laughing are two different things. Joy is something within. Our Lord was full of joy. Even when He was rejected by Capernaum and Corazin and all those places, He could turn His heart to the Lord and say, "Lord, I praise You because this is Your will hidden from the prudent and the wise but revealed to the babes." He was full of joy.

Some people said, "You are *the* prophet that Moses prophesied of in Deuteronomy: One day there will be one among you raised up by God, and whatever that prophet says, if you rebel against him and disobey him you shall perish." Some said He is *the* prophet.

But the Lord was not satisfied. He asked His disciples: "Whom do you say that I am? You have been with Me for three years. Whom do you say that I am?" And you remember Peter said, "You are the Christ, the Son of the living God."

And the Lord said, "Blessed are you Simon Bar-jona, this is not something shown you by flesh and blood. It is My heavenly Father who reveals it to you. You are Peter. You have become a stone and I will build My church upon this rock, and the gates of Hades shall not prevail against it" (see Matthew 16:16-18). What a revelation!

After that revelation the Lord began to reveal to His disciples for the first time: "I am going to Jerusalem. I will be rejected, I will be scourged, and I will be put to death, but on the third day I will rise again." You remember what Peter did?

Peter took hold of the Lord and said, "Lord, don't do it! Never! This is not necessary. You can have the world without giving up Your soul." And the Lord turned around and said, "Satan, get behind Me." This was not Peter. This was Satan. "Because you do not mind the things of God, you only mind the things of man." You see man's concept of value.

THE VALUE OF THE CROSS

It is very true. Because of the sin of the world, because of our fallen soul, the only way that our Lord can redeem us back to true value has to be the cross. He will not be the Christ if He does not go to the cross. You cannot have a crossless Christ because without the cross, He cannot fulfill the mission for which the Father sent Him into this world. The Father did not send Him into this world just to demonstrate to the world what a true man really is—a man after God's heart, a man of God's original design, a man that knows true value and expresses true value. If it was only a demonstration, then on the mount of transfiguration He could have exited from this world because He had the right to go to the Father, but then there would be only one man in heaven. In order to deliver our soul, in order to bring us back to true value, our Lord Jesus had to go to the cross. There on the cross, not only were our sins being borne by our Lord, our sins forgiven because of His shed blood, but it was on the cross that His soul was poured out like water. He gave up His soul. On the cross, our old man was crucified with Him. This soul of man that has fallen, that has every value distorted, has to go through the cross to death, and out of that comes resurrection, the glorious life of the risen Lord.

The Lord has already accomplished the work of salvation. In other words, it is finished. So when we come to the Lord, not only our sins are forgiven but our old man was crucified with Him. That is why the apostle Paul can say, "I am crucified with Christ. *I* am crucified with Christ. No longer live I, but it is Christ who lives in me, and I now live in the flesh by faith; not my faith but the faith of the Son of God who loved me and gave Himself for me" (see Galatians 2:20).

BEING RESTORED TO GOD'S VALUE

We who have believed in the Lord Jesus, we who have His blood sprinkled, cleansing our conscience, we who have been saved, we who have His life in us, who have His Spirit in us, our problem now is that if we still continue to live by our old flesh, which is possible, then our whole sense of value will be upside down. I sometimes think as Christians, mentally we all understand that spiritual value is more important than physical things. We all know that, but the problem is: How will it work? We know it but it does not work. It seems as if we are knowingly going in the wrong direction. The world still has such attraction, such power upon us, and it is working against us spiritually. It is still demanding our soul, and we are still giving in. It is a strange situation. How can we be fully restored to the value that God has set? Or to put it this way: How can we really value God above all things? Here is the secret. The Lord said, "He that loses his life for My sake shall gain it. He that shall gain his soul-life shall lose it. Deny yourself, take up your cross, and follow Me. Otherwise, you cannot be My disciples."

SEEING THE GLORY OF THE LORD

The work is done, the possibility is there, the power is there, but we need to respond by faith. But again, unless the Lord opens our eyes and gives us a glimpse of His glory we will not be able to let go of ourselves. If only we can see Him in His glory, then we will be able to let go of ourselves. Otherwise, if we do not see the unseen, for us to deny ourselves is impossible.

This is true in the Old Testament as well as in the New Testament time, as we see with Abraham. Because the Lord of glory appeared to him, that enabled him to leave his native place and his kindred and go to the place where God had called him. As a matter of fact, in Hebrews chapter 11, the New Testament explained to us what Abraham did. In Genesis all we can see is that he left Ur of Chaldea because the glory of the Lord attracted him. He obeyed the Lord and went to Canaan, the promised land, even though, throughout his life, he was just a sojourner there, and yet he believed that God had promised and God would fulfill it and give him the land and also the seed. But in the New Testament we find that his faith actually goes further than that because our Lord Jesus said, "Abraham saw My day and he was glad." In other words, Abraham saw in the seed of Isaac even the days of Christ, and Abraham was not seeking for an earthly piece of land; he was waiting for that city with foundation whose builder is God. He was already looking forward to the new Jerusalem. How could he do that? It is because the glory of the Lord appeared to him. That enabled him to despise the temporary, earthly things and to seek that which is spiritual and eternal, the true value.

The same thing is true with Moses. The Bible says that Moses would rather suffer shame, reproach with God's people than to enjoy all the riches of Egypt because he had seen the unseen.

We need to ask the Lord to really give us a sight of Himself. If we see Him then the things of this world will grow strangely dim in the light of His glory and grace. So it is not something that as Christians we try not to love the world or try to be ascetic. No; it is because we have seen the Lord, and seeing Him we cannot but follow Him.

Then you will discover when you really seek the Lord as your true value, everything will return to its normal order, even in eating and drinking. Now do not think that because you are spiritual and seeking spiritual things, therefore you do not eat and you do not drink. Our Lord Jesus was on earth and He ate and drank, even with the sinners and taxgathers. The Pharisees said, "Now You, the holy Man, how do You do that?"

Even the disciples of John had an argument and came to the Lord and said, "Why is it that Your disciples do not fast?" It is true, if your sense of value is not corrected, that is, if you do not see the value of the spiritual, the value of God, then all these physical, earthly things will work against you. They become lusts; they become something deadening your life. But if you really let the Lord be your true value, your true treasure, you will eat and drink to the glory of God. Even all of these earthly things will fall into their right place. They will not be against you but they will be supporting you. Value will be restored to its order.

TRUE VALUE IS ACCORDING TO PURPOSE

Value is according to purpose. God has a purpose and it is out of that purpose that He created all things. He created man according to that purpose, and that purpose is that all things will be summed up in Christ Jesus, in His Son. That is the purpose. So whenever it is something that is in line with His purpose, there is value, true value. If there is anything that is out of that line, no matter how good it may look, it has no value, no eternal value. On the contrary, it may have negative value. So it is important in our lives to see this purpose.

We are not created for ourselves; we are created for Him. God has created us for our Lord Jesus. We are to be His bride. It is not good for man to be alone. God said, "I will make him a help meet, His like." We are to be His like. We are to be like Him, so that we can be joined to Him and be His satisfaction, His fulfillment. That is purpose; that is the purpose of our life. Every day we live, we live for that purpose; everything we do, we do it with that purpose in view. Why do I eat? Why do I drink? It is that I may live for Him. The way we use our time, the way we do our job, the way we live in our family, the way we live in the church, the way we live in this world is for that purpose. Everything that will add to that purpose has value. Your days are not wasted. But if a day is not adding to that purpose, it is a wasted day.

The Lord is coming soon. We do not have much time to waste. It is time for us to wake up. It is time for us to seize upon true value, spiritual value.

Let us pray:

Lord, we do acknowledge that words are useless unless Thou speakest. Lord, we pray that Thou wilt speak to each of our hearts that we may not only know mentally but that experientially we will really seek only Thee because all spiritual value is in Thee. May our every day count for eternity and may Thou be glorified. We ask in the name of our Lord Jesus. Amen

SPIRITUAL VALUE IN PRACTICE

Philippians 3:7-8—But what things were gain to me these I counted, on account of Christ, loss. But surely I count also all things to be loss on account of the excellency of the knowledge of Christ Jesus my Lord, on account of whom I have suffered the loss of all, and count them to be filth, that I may gain Christ.

Shall we pray:

Dear Lord, our hearts do bow in worship. We praise and thank Thee for Thy amazing love towards us. Lord, we do desire to be so constrained by Thy love that we will not live again for ourselves but only for Thee, the One who loved us and gave Himself for us. Lord, as we continue in Thy presence we ask that Thou will, by Thy Holy Spirit, once again open our eyes that we may see the value of Thyself. Lord, Thou art more valuable, much more incomparable to anything in this world. Lord, give us that desire to gain Christ even to the loss of all things. We commit this time into

Thy hands and trust Thy Holy Spirit to guide our thoughts. We ask in the name of our Lord Jesus. Amen.

God's valuation is very different from ours, and it is God who decides, determines value, not ourselves. Strangely, when we look at value from our own experience, it varies with different people. One may look at a thing as very valuable and is willing to pay a high price for it but the very same thing may be of little value or even of no value to another person. It is as if value is determined by the beholder. Because of this, things on this earth, so far as value is concerned, are all relative. There is no absolute thing in this world. As human beings, in our eyes, everything is relative, but we know that the one who determines value is not us; it is God. God Himself is the supreme value, and He invested certain values in the things that He created. As a matter of fact, value is that measure of God in a thing or in a person. If there are more manifestations of God, of His glory, of His wisdom, of His character, then that thing or that person has more value. But if a thing does not manifest God in His glory, wisdom, power, or character, then no matter what that thing or who that person is, spiritually speaking, there is no value.

When God creates things, He puts value in everything because everything comes out of His hand. The created things show us the divinity and the power of God, and that is their value. Human beings were created in the image of God; therefore human beings are more valuable than other created things. But today, because sin has entered into this world, this whole matter of value, so far as we are concerned, is all distorted, upside down. The Bible says the natural man does not receive the things of God because they are folly to him and he cannot know them because they are spiritually discerned. So far as human beings are concerned, so far as our natural man is concerned, we are not really able to see clearly what value really is, where is value, or what is more valuable. Sin has blinded our eyes.

In John 9, our Lord Jesus healed a man born blind. Because He did it on the Sabbath, the Pharisees were angry and they even cast that blind man who was healed out of the synagogue.

They excommunicated him because he was healed by the Lord on the Sabbath. The Bible says that the Lord found him. The Lord knew he was excommunicated, so the Lord went to find him and asked him if he believed the Son of God. And the man said, "Who is He that I might believe?" The Lord said, "The one who is talking with you." And he bowed down and worshiped the Lord. Then the Lord said something, "They who see continue in sin but the blind are healed." When the Pharisees heard about it, they said, "Are you saying that we are blind?" And the Lord said, "If you are blind then you can see, but because you say you can see, your sin remains with you."

If we think we see, if we think we know what value really is, we continue in sin, but if we come to the point that we realize we are blind, that we have been blinded by the god of this world, then we have the chance to really see, to know what real value is.

Our Lord Jesus came into this world not only to teach us what real value is, He also demonstrated it in His own life. Throughout His life His sense of valuation is totally different from that of the world, and that is the reason why people just could not understand Him. Even His disciples could not understand Him because His way of valuing things was so different from everybody. But thank God, not only did He come to teach and to demonstrate true value, He also came to restore us to true value. So it is by the cross that He restored us, and through the cross He brings us into true, spiritual value.

We would like to use a person's life to illustrate that principle. We have talked about spiritual value in principle, but now we would like to share together on spiritual value in practice, to see how this matter of spiritual value is solved in a person's life. Of course, immediately, you know we are talking about Paul. So we would like to review about Paul.

PAUL'S CREDENTIALS

Formerly, this man Paul was named Saul. He was named after the first king in Israel. Saul was born in Tarsus, a Gentile city, but he was born a Roman and he was a freeman. During his days it was the Roman Empire. The Romans had conquered the world and they had more slaves than freemen. Those who were conquered by the Romans were slaves. Only the Romans were freemen, but there were certain cities or certain people that were given the privilege of Roman citizenship and Saul was born free. He was born a Roman with privileges of a Roman citizen, and in that time, this was a tremendous thing. In other words, he was politically correct.

He was born with Roman citizenship and he was born in Tarsus. During that time, even though politically it belonged to Rome, culturally, it belonged to Greeks. In other words, the Greek culture was the culture of those days. So when Saul grew up, he received Greek culture. He knew Greek philosophy. He was brought up in that kind of environment, and it was a thing to boast of. So we may say he was culturally correct—not a barbarian.

He said he was of the race of Israel, of the tribe of Benjamin, and on the eighth day he was circumcised. In other words, he was a typical Jew. He was not like Ishmael. Ishmael was circumcised at sixteen, but God's ordained time for circumcision for the children of Abraham is the eighth day. On the eighth day, a male child has to be circumcised and Saul was circumcised on the eighth day.

He was of the tribe of Benjamin. When Israel was divided into two parts, the northern ten tribes became the nation of Israel and the southern tribe of Judah, together with the tribe of Benjamin, became the nation of Judah. In other words, he belonged to that nation that had never been divided out from the original one.

He was a Hebrew of Hebrews. What does that mean? We are told that a Hebrew of Hebrews means that he was not only born in a Hebrew family but in that family their spoken language was Hebrew. In other words, many were born in the Hebrew families living outside the promised land. Because they were surrounded by Greek culture, they did not speak Hebrew in the family. They spoke Greek or other dialects, but Saul belonged to a family that spoke Hebrew in the family. So it was very kosher, very correct. So you find that he was racially correct.

During those days, at the age of twelve, a boy would go through the ceremony of bar mitzvah, and that boy became a son of the law. In other words, he was considered as grown up and he was now responsible for his actions. He became a member of the synagogue and he had the right to ask questions and also to answer questions. Saul went to Jerusalem to receive religious education. So maybe, when he was twelve, he was taken to Jerusalem, and there he was to learn the law under a famous rabbi, Gamaliel. He sat under the feet of Gamaliel and he learned all about the law, about Judaism. He received all the traditions of the fathers, all the teachings of the rabbis through the centuries. He was well educated, so he was religiously correct.

PAUL'S PURSUIT OF VALUE

Everything with Paul was correct. Even though he was rather young, he sought after what he considered as things of more value. Young men with that kind of background would probably seek after earthly, worldly things because he had every opportunity before him. But this young man was different. Somehow he felt that spiritual things (to him he thought they were spiritual things), that is religious things, were more valuable than earthly things. That was most unusual. While other young people were seeking after positions, fame, wealth, and all these earthly, worldly things, this young man sought after things religious because he considered this matter of the soul was more important than physical, material things. And he really pursued it with determination. He was a young man of strong will and he was determined that he would become someone in Judaism. Some people have said that at a young age he had already became a member of the Sanhedrin because when the believers of the Lord Jesus, the followers of the Lord were sentenced, he gave his vote. But other people said it could not be because he was too young for that and he was not married. To be a member of the Sanhedrin you had to be married. This is something we do not know and there are different opinions about it.

He himself told us he was more advanced in Judaism that his contemporaries. He was seeking for the top place in Judaism. He could have been *the* rabbi of his time, and he thought these things were important, these things were valuable. And he was very moral because he said, "I am a Pharisee of the Pharisees, a true Pharisee."

You remember when our Lord was upon earth the one class of person to whom He proclaimed His woes was the Pharisees: "Woe to you, Pharisees and scribes." Why? It is because they were hypocrites. Outwardly, they kept all the minute things of the law and yet, inwardly, they violated every bit of it. They were hypocrites. When they prayed they would stand at the corner of the street and pray long prayers so everybody would say, "How godly that person must be." Hypocrites! But not this young man. He was a true Pharisee because he could even boast and say, "According to the law I am righteous." He tried to keep every letter of the law with sincerity. We would say this young man is unusual; he must have found the secret of value. Because of that, he persecuted the followers of Jesus. To him, according to the tradition of the fathers, he considered Jesus as an impostor of Judaism. Jesus did not conform to the traditions of the fathers. They considered Jesus as a rebel and must be ridden.

So you find this young man was very zealous for Judaism, very zealous for the tradition of the fathers. As a matter of fact, we can say the tradition of the fathers in Judaism at that time was the best tradition in the world. So he persecuted the followers of the Lord Jesus with zeal. He would enter into houses and seize men and women and children and condemn them. When Stephen, the first martyr, was martyred, he was there watching the clothes of those who stoned Stephen to death. Usually, a moral person would not do anything to the women or children, but that zeal blinded him so much that he would go into the houses and seize not only men but women and children. He even received documents from the high priest to go into the Gentile cities outside of Palestine proper and try to seize believers of Jesus and bring them to Jerusalem in order to condemn them. Now that was Saul.

Why did he do all these things? It is because value determines your life. You will seek after what you value. This young man's sense of value was such that he valued very highly his pedigree. He valued very much that he was a Jew, and an orthodox Jew. He valued his upbringing. He valued his knowledge of the law. He valued his own moral achievements, and he valued religious success. He valued these things. He wanted to be someone in Judaism because he thought that was valuable.

Whatever you value will determine what kind of life you will live and it will decide how much you are willing to pay for it. This young man paid a lot for what he valued. Probably, when other young men were seeking the pleasure of this world, he was diligently studying the law, interpreting the law, and so forth. He paid a great cost for the things that he valued, and he was nearly successful in what he was seeking. That was Saul.

SAUL'S ENCOUNTER WITH THE LORD JESUS

So far as the world is concerned, I think the whole world would admire such a person. The whole world would say, "This young man is right." One day he was on the way to Damascus, a Gentile city in Syria, with documents from the high priest to seize the people of the Way, those who believed in the Lord Jesus, to bring them to Jerusalem to sentence them. But thank God, as he was approaching the city of Damascus at noon time, the Bible tells us (This experience is recorded three times in the book of Acts.) that suddenly, a light brighter than the sun shone upon him and his followers and they all fell on the ground. That light was so powerful it struck them to the ground and then he heard a voice speaking in Hebrew: "Saul, Saul, why do you persecute Me? It is hard for you to kick against the goads."

We think that we are free persons and we can do anything that we want. We are not born slaves; we are born free men. We can live our own lives and seek what we think is valuable for us. But according to the word of God, this is not the case. God has a purpose for each one of us. Even before the foundation of the world He has chosen us in Christ Jesus. When we were in our mother's womb, He had already separated us for that purpose. We do not know it. Saul did not know it, but the Lord said, "It is hard for you to kick against the goads." Now we know what the goads are. During the old days when they did farming, they would have an ox under yoke. The farmer would put his hand on the plow and plow the field with the ox, but the ox sometimes had his own will and would not follow the will of his master. During the plowing, maybe the ox would see something nice to eat and he would begin to turn and the furrow would not be straight. So the farmer would take a stick with a sharp end called a goad and just touch the leg of the ox. Now of course the farmer had no intention of hurting the ox because he wanted to use him. He just touched it lightly to remind the ox that he had a master and he did not want him to forget it. But the ox was so stubborn that when the goad touched him, he kicked back. When he kicked back, it hurt, and because it hurt he learned. Then he knew that he had to listen to his master; otherwise he would be hurt more.

The Lord was saying to this young man Saul: You are not free. Even before the foundation of the world I have chosen you. In your mother's womb I have separated you, but you do not know it. You are created with a purpose. You are to do My will, to plow My field, to do My work, not your work. You have a Master, but you forgot. You thought that you could do anything you like. You thought that you could determine what value is. I will let you go just so far but I have touched you with the goads, but you do not understand.

I believe this young man, while he was persecuting the followers of Jesus, while he was seizing upon those people, being a moral being, a good man so far as the world was concerned, from time to time, he must have seen the way those believers reacted. It must have touched his conscience, especially in the case of Stephen. When Stephen gave his testimony, people looked at him and saw his face shine like an angel, and Saul was there. He heard what Stephen said and he was with the people who pushed Stephen out of the city. When Stephen was stoned, he said that he saw the heaven opened and the Son of Man standing there waiting, welcoming him. When he was dying, he said, "Lord, do not put this sin upon them." Being a true Pharisee, a moral person, he could not but be deeply touched. The death of Stephen was like a goad touching his leg. His conscience must have been bothered, but he kicked back.

According to the book of Acts, after the death of Stephen, you find that Saul became mad. He was furious. He persecuted the followers of the Lord even more than before. Why is it? He tried to silence his conscience. So the Lord reminded him: It is hard for you to kick against the goads. How long are you going to kick against the goads? You only hurt yourself.

For the first time Saul realized that he was not his own master, that he had a Master. There is One who is stronger than he. For the first time his inner eyes were opened. He said, "Lord, who are You? I do not know You, but I acknowledge You are Lord because You are mightier. I cannot fight against You. Now who are You?" And a voice said, "I am Jesus whom you persecuted."

At that moment his evaluation of Jesus completely changed. Before he saw the Lord, before the Lord spoke to him, he thought he could see. He thought he saw clearly his way, his future. He knew what value was, and he looked at Jesus as the Nazarene, the one to be despised, the one to be away with, the one to be crucified, to be wiped out, annihilated, destroyed. He looked down upon Jesus. He trampled upon Jesus. That was his evaluation of Jesus. But at that moment his whole evaluation of Jesus changed. He saw that Jesus is Lord. He is his Master. He is God. He has chosen him even before the foundation of the world. He knew him even when he was in his mother's womb. He was so patient waiting for him, working on him, until one day his inner eyes were opened and he began to see the risen Lord, the Lord of all. What a change in his estimation of the Person of Jesus! And that vision transformed his sense of value.

PAUL'S CHANGED SENSE OF VALUE

Paul himself testified in Philippians 3 that in the past he boasted of his birth, his privilege, his achievement, his moral status, and his zeal. In other words, he boasted of himself, of his flesh. He thought highly of himself. He thought he was a man above others, that he was on the right track, that he had seized the true value of life. But when he met Jesus or when Jesus met him, his whole sense of value changed—downside up.

He said: What I considered as gain, now, on account of Christ Jesus, I look at these as loss. My pedigree, my education, my achievement, my zeal, all these things were gain to me in the past, but now I see clearly they are actually loss because they blinded my eyes to see real value. I wasted my energy, my pursuit, my time, my life, on something that is not worth a thing. And all the time I thought these were gain, but they were actually loss.

He went a step further. He said, "I not only count these former things that I had as loss now, I count all things as loss for the excellency of the knowledge of Jesus Christ." Once he saw the Lord Jesus, he saw the glory of the Lord Jesus, it changed his whole mentality. The whole world was like filth to him. Now who wants filth? The quicker you get rid of it the better. But the knowledge of Jesus Christ, to know Jesus Christ is the most valuable thing in the whole world.

Has our sense of value changed? When we are saved, our sense of value should change; and I believe that there must be some change. It may not be drastic but there ought to be some change. If there is no change in your sense of value, I wonder whether you are really saved. But unfortunately, even though there was some change in our sense of value when we were saved, the change is not drastic enough. Because of that, you find the things of old continue to cling upon us, continue to have influence upon us; and unfortunately, they will overwhelm that new sense of value and lead us to walk in the old way of life. We do not see the value of our Lord Jesus as we should.

PAUL'S DESIRE TO KNOW THE LORD

In the case of Paul, because he saw the glory of the Lord, that glory made everything dim. He would rather lose everything if he can gain Christ. He began to see how God sees. He began to value the way God values. God values His Son more than anything else, and when you begin to value Christ more than anything else, you want to know Him. In order to know Him, you are willing to pay any price, you are willing to look at everything as dross. You are on the right track. You have the true value.

Paul said, "I want to know Him." In the past he was building up his own righteousness. According to the righteousness of the law he said, "I am perfect; I am blameless." But our righteousnesses before God are as filthy rags. No one can be justified by keeping the law and Saul was included. He was blinded. He thought that he could build up his own righteousness to face God, but there on the road to Damascus his own righteousnesses appeared as filthy rags. Thank God, God took off his filthy rags and put upon him the best robe. So he said, "Now it is the righteousness of God through Christ Jesus by faith." Paul realized he had no righteousness of his own. He was naked before God and Christ was his robe. He was clothed with Christ. That gave him standing before the righteous God. Thank God, this is what the cross of our Lord Jesus has done for us. He bore our sins in His own body on the tree. He who knew no sin was made sin for us that we may be the righteousness of God. Thank God, we are justified. The blood has cleansed us and we can stand before God. But Paul said, "It is not just this work of our Lord Jesus on the cross that gives me righteousness, a righteous standing before God that I treasure; I want to know Him. I want to know the Person who did so much for me."

We know some of the works of our Lord Jesus. We know His finished work on the cross, and because we know the finished work of Christ on the cross, we know our sins are forgiven, we know that we now have the righteousness of God upon us, we know now that we have a standing before God. Thank God, we know the work of our Lord Jesus. We treasure His work and we should, but we treasure His work more than we treasure the Person.

Paul said, "Because I have received His work in my life, I want to know the Person who gave me such grace. I want to know Him." Do we have such a desire in us to know Him and not just to know His work? Of course, we must know His work, but we need to know Him—His Person. We need to know His character, know His mind, know His will, know what He really loves, what He wants, how to please Him.

The apostle Paul in II Corinthians 5 said, "I have an ambition and my ambition is that in all things I may be agreeable to Him, or that I may please Him in all things. That is my ambition: I want to know Him." Do we have such a strong desire to know Him? Of course, to know Him you have to be close to Him, to have a daily, living relationship with Him in order to know Him, to know the power of His resurrection.

When we begin to know Him, we know that He is not only our Savior, we know He is our life. It is more than Him coming to save us out of sin, out of death into eternal life. It is Christ in you, the hope of glory. Christ is your life. When you begin to know Him, you begin to know His life, His life in you. But His life is resurrection life. When Christ was crucified, He took the old man with Him and in Him you were crucified. Unless we are willing to see that there is no good in our flesh, we have no confidence in our old life, we will not live again by our old life, but by the Holy Spirit we will deliver it unto death on the cross, we will not really know Christ, our life. In other words, we will not live by His life; we are still living by our old life. How many believers are still living by their old life! The reason they are not able to live by the Christ life in them is because they are not willing to let go of their old life. They still have confidence in their flesh. They still feel they can live a Christian life by themselves. Not until you come to the point that you realize in you, that is in your flesh there is no good and you let go and accept the sentence of death from the Lord, do you begin to experience Christ, your life. The life is there and it gives opportunity for Christ to live in you, and when He lives, it is resurrection life, it is the power of His resurrection. You are living on a different realm and being conformed to have fellowship with His sufferings.

The sufferings of our Lord on the cross are two kinds. One kind we call vicarious or atoning suffering, and that suffering He suffered alone. He alone bore our sins in His body and trod the winepress. He atoned for our sins. You and I cannot participate in that suffering. We only receive the benefit of that suffering. But there is another kind of suffering of our Lord Jesus that we are called to have fellowship with, to share with Him. It is to suffer for righteousness sake. It is to suffer for the will of God. It is to suffer for following the Lord, to suffer for lost souls, to suffer for the house of God, the church. As Paul said he travailed in suffering in order to complete that which is behind of the afflictions of Christ for His body. In that area we are called to share with Him. But it is only when we begin to know the power of His resurrection that we are able to fellowship with His sufferings. Otherwise, we will not be able to share with His sufferings.

"Conformed to His death." That goes deeper because we know the death of our Lord Jesus is all-inclusive. It is death to everything that is of the old creation, everything that is not of God. We are to be conformed to that death. Whatever in our life is not of God, no matter how good it may look, we are to be conformed to that death so that Christ may be all and in all to us. This is something the apostle Paul is pursuing after. He considered this as the supreme value. He said, "I do not say I have already arrived. No, I am still pressing on, forgetting the things that are behind and pursuing the goal. I want to apprehend all that Christ has apprehended me for." He wanted to gain that prize, and that prize is Christ, to gain Him in His fulness.

Here you find a person whose whole sense of value was corrected. It changed his whole course of life, and to the very end he could say, "I have finished my course, I have kept the faith, I have fought the good fight. Now there is a crown of righteousness waiting for me; but not only for me, but for all who love His appearing."

Brothers and sisters, is this what we are seeking today? Has our sense of value been completely changed? How we need continually to see the glory of the Lord! If we have His glory before us, it will enable us to forget everything and just follow Him, seeking after Him. This is true value. All things will pass away but Jesus forever. So may the Lord help us.

Let us pray:

Dear heavenly Father, we do thank Thee that Thou has shown us it is possible, and Thou has made it possible to change the sense of value in a person so completely that he may see exactly the way that You see. Lord, because of this we are encouraged. We are here. We do acknowledge that once we were blind but now we see, but Lord, sometimes we see dimly. We need a further touch of Your hand that we may see clearly the excellency of the knowledge of Jesus Christ, that we may count all things but filth. We want to gain Thee. Thou art the only one worthy to seek after. Oh Lord, have mercy upon us. We ask in Thy precious name. Amen.

.

Other Books Printed By
Christian Testimony Ministry

Speaker	Title
Dana Congdon	Marriage, Singleness, and the Will of God
	Recovery & Restoration
	The Holy Spirit
	Hebrews
A.J. Flack	Tent of His Splendour
Stephen Kaung	Acts
	Be Ye Therefore Perfect
	Called Out Unto Christ
	Called to the Fellowship of God's Son
	Divine Life and Order
	For Me to Live is Christ
	Glorious Liberty of the Children of God
	God's Purpose for the Family
	I Will Build My Church
	Meditations on the Kingdom
	Recovery
	Spiritual Exercise
	Spiritual Life (II Corinthians Series)
	Teach Us to Pray
	The Cross
	The Fulness of Christ—In the Book of Revelation
	The Headship of Christ
	The Kingdom and the Church
	The Kingdom of God
	The Last Call to the Churches, the Call to Overcome
	The Life of Our Lord Jesus
	The Life of the Church, the Body of Christ
	The Lord's Table
	Two Guideposts for Inheriting the Kingdom
	Vision of Christ (Revelation)
	Who Are We?

WHY DO WE SO GATHER?
WORSHIP

LANCE LAMBERT

CALLED UNTO HIS ETERNAL GLORY
GOD'S ETERNAL PURPOSE
IN THE DAY OF THY POWER
JACOB I HAVE LOVED
LIVING FAITH
LESSONS FROM THE LIFE OF MOSES
LOVE DIVINE
MY HOUSE SHALL BE A HOUSE OF PRAYER
PREPARATION FOR THE COMING OF THE LORD
REIGNING WITH CHRIST
SPIRITUAL CHARACTER
THE GOSPEL OF THE KINGDOM
THE IMPORTANCE OF COVERING
THE LAST DAYS AND GOD'S PRIORITIES
THE PRIZE
THE SUPREMACY OF JESUS CHRIST
THINE IS THE POWER!
THOU ART MINE

T. AUSTIN-SPARKS

THE LORD'S TESTIMONY AND THE WORLD NEED

HARVEY CEDARS CONFERENCE

STEPHEN KAUNG

HEAVENLY VISION
SPIRITUAL RESPONSIBILITY

CONGDON, HILE, KAUNG

SPIRITUAL MINISTRY
SPIRITUAL AUTHORITY
SPIRITUAL HOUSE
SPIRITUAL SUBMISSION

STEPHEN KAUNG

SPIRITUAL KNOWLEDGE
SPIRITUAL POWER
SPIRITUAL REALITY
SPIRITUAL VALUE
SPIRITUAL BLESSING
SPIRITUAL DISCERNMENT